PRESIDENTS OF THE U.S.A.

GROVER CLEVELAND
OUR TWENTY-SECOND AND
TWENTY-FOURTH PRESIDENT

by Ann Graham Gaines

THE CHILD'S WORLD ®

Published in the United States of America

The Child's World®
1980 Lookout Drive • Mankato, MN 56003-1705
800-599-READ • www.childsworld.com

Acknowledgments
The Child's World®: Mary Berendes, Publishing Director

The Creative Spark: Mary McGavic, Project Director; Shari Joffe, Editorial
Director; Deborah Goodsite, Photo Research; Nancy Ratkiewich, Page Production

The Design Lab: Kathleen Petelinsek, Design

Content Adviser: Sharon Farrell, Grover Cleveland Birthplace, Caldwell, New Jersey

Photos
Cover and page 3: White House Historical Association (White House Collection)
(detail); White House Historical Association (White House Collection)

Interior: Alamy: 5 and 38 (James Nesterwitz), 31 (North Wind Picture Archives);
The Art Archive: 16, 19 (Culver Pictures); Art Resource, NY: 22, 24 (National
Portrait Gallery, Smithsonian Institution) (detail); Benjamin Harrison Presidential
Site: 23; City of Buffalo Arts Commission (New York) Mayoral Portrait
Commission: 14; Corbis: 11, 27 (Corbis), 21 (C. M. Bell), 25 and 39, 32, 36
(Bettmann), 26 (Museum of the City of New York); Courtesy of the Buffalo and
Erie County Historical Society: 35; Courtesy of NJ Division of Parks and Forestry,
State Park Service, Grover Cleveland Birthplace State Historic Site: 8, 33; The
Granger Collection, New York: 15, 20, 37; The Image Works: 4 (Roger-Viollet);
iStockphoto: 44 (Tim Fan); Library of Congress: 17, 18, 28 and 38; The New
Jersey State Archives; Department of State: 6, 7, 10; North Wind Picture Archives:
9, 29 (North Wind); Picture History: 13; Princeton University Library: 34; U.S. Air
Force photo: 45.

Library of Congress Cataloging-in-Publication Data
Gaines, Ann.
  Grover Cleveland / by Ann Graham Gaines.
     p. cm.— (Presidents of the U.S.A.)
  Includes bibliographical references and index.
  ISBN 978-1-60253-051-5 (library bound : alk. paper)
  1. Cleveland, Grover, 1837–1908—Juvenile literature. 2. Presidents—United
States—Biography—Juvenile literature. I. Title. II. Series.

  E697.G34 2008
  973.8'5092—dc22
  [B]

                              2007049066

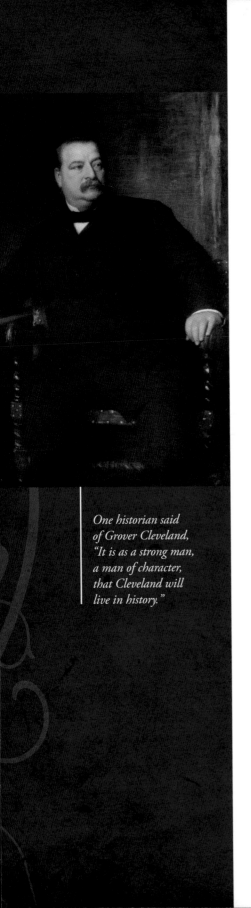

One historian said
of Grover Cleveland,
"It is as a strong man,
a man of character,
that Cleveland will
live in history."

TABLE OF CONTENTS

CHAPTER ONE

THE EARLY YEARS

When Grover Cleveland was elected in 1884, he became the 22nd president of the United States. When he was not reelected in 1888, many Americans thought his political career was over. But Grover Cleveland proved them wrong, when he was once again elected in 1892, becoming the nation's twenty-fourth president. To this day, he is the only president who served two terms that were not **consecutive**—that did not come one right after the other.

Stephen Grover Cleveland was born on March 18, 1837, in Caldwell, New Jersey. He always went by his middle name, Grover. His parents were Richard and Ann Cleveland. Theirs was a large and lively family. Grover was the fifth of their nine children.

Richard Cleveland was a Presbyterian minister. He was a friendly man, and the people of his church admired him. Ann Cleveland was also well liked by

President Grover Cleveland was known for his honesty and for his willingness to work hard.

the community. When not taking care of her own family, she helped her husband by visiting the sick and cooking meals for the needy. Like many ministers' families, the Cleveland family never had much money.

The Clevelands moved during Grover's childhood, from Caldwell, New Jersey, to the small town of Fayetteville, New York. Later they moved to Clinton and finally Holland Patent, New York. Wherever the Clevelands lived, their home was a happy, busy place where the children did chores and played games together. They also enjoyed school. Grover Cleveland was always

Stephen Grover Cleveland was born in this house in the small town of Caldwell, New Jersey. At the time, most babies were born at home, usually without help from a doctor.

As a little boy, Grover Cleveland was once almost run over by a runaway horse and wagon. A passerby rescued him.

Visitors to Grover Cleveland's New Jersey birthplace (now a state historic site) can see the cradle he slept in as a baby.

Reverend Richard Cleveland was a minister in Caldwell when his son Grover was born. Grover's family was deeply religious. Each Saturday night was spent giving all the Cleveland children baths in preparation for church the next day.

a good student, although he was never the best in his class. He earned good grades by working hard.

As a teenager, Grover Cleveland hoped that even though his family did not have a lot of money, he would get to go to college. This would not happen, however. When Grover was 16, his father died. Suddenly, Ann Cleveland was left alone to provide for her family. There were few jobs available for women in Holland Patent at the time. Besides, Ann was needed at home. She still had to cook, clean, and tend to the four children who were younger than Grover.

To help his family out, Grover dropped out of high school. He went to work to earn money. On his own, he traveled to New York City. His older brother William worked there, at a school for the blind. William helped Grover get his own teaching job there. Grover Cleveland proved himself a good teacher. He found his new job interesting. But he became so homesick for his family that he soon moved back to Holland Patent.

At the age of 18, Grover ventured into the world again. He boarded a train intending to travel to

Ann Cleveland was responsible for the well-being of her children after her husband died in 1853. Grover was 16 years old at the time. To help support the family, he left school to find work.

Ohio, but stopped to visit relatives in Buffalo, New York. They asked him to stay a while. For a time he worked on his uncle's farm. By this time, Grover was a tall, strong man who could work for many hours at a time.

Grover liked living with his relatives and working on the farm. But when a family friend offered him a job at his law office, he accepted. Grover could earn much more as a law clerk than as a farmhand. His mother still needed him to help pay the family's bills, so the increase in pay was important.

Soon Grover realized he would like to be not just a clerk, but a real lawyer. Today most people become lawyers by attending law school. There they prepare to take the bar exam, which one must pass to become

This rare photograph shows Grover Cleveland (far left) with almost all of his brothers and sisters. One sister was not able to be present for the photograph.

When he was 17, Cleveland was offered a scholarship to a Presbyterian college. It would have paid for his education to become a minister like his father. Grover longed for an education, but he could not take advantage of this opportunity. His family needed him to earn money to help support them.

a lawyer. But Grover Cleveland could not go to law school because he did not have a high-school diploma or a college degree. Instead, he taught himself the law. He spent all his free time studying for the bar exam. Spending many hours every day and night at his desk meant he had little exercise. Grover had always loved to eat and drink, but he also had been physically active, too. Without exercise, he began to gain weight.

In 1859, thanks to hard work and determination, Grover passed the bar exam and became a lawyer. He accepted a new job in the same law office where he had worked as a clerk.

The years when Grover Cleveland was a young man were difficult ones for the United States. The

Civil War broke out in 1861. Eleven southern states seceded—or left—the United States and formed a new country, the Confederate States of America. Grover Cleveland believed that the **Union,** those states that remained, was right in fighting to force the rebelling states back into the Union. But he did not join the Union army. His family still needed his financial support, so he continued to pursue what

Cleveland was interested in **politics** from the time he first arrived in Buffalo. During elections, he would walk around town reminding people to vote.

Cleveland traveled to Buffalo after his father died. He remained in the city for the next 28 years, winning increasingly important positions in city and state government.

Grover Cleveland paid a Polish **immigrant** named George Beninski to fight for him in the Civil War. Beninski survived the war.

was turning out to be a very successful law career. In 1863, Grover was **appointed** assistant district attorney for Erie County, New York. This meant he now worked for the county as a lawyer. He took evidence collected by sheriffs and their deputies. He then went to court and tried to prove that people accused of crimes were guilty.

This photograph shows Grover Cleveland at age 26, when he was the assistant district attorney of Erie County. As a young man, Cleveland was slim, strong, and handsome. He enjoyed food a great deal, however. By the time he was president, he weighed more than 250 pounds (113 kg).

CIVIL WAR SUBSTITUTES

Cleveland had just begun to earn a **reputation** as a good lawyer when the Civil War began in 1861. The Union army needed many new soldiers. At first, thousands of men like those shown above volunteered to fight. But as the war continued, fewer people volunteered. The country started to draft soldiers. This means it could require young men of a certain age to join the army.

At the time, the law allowed a man to pay someone to serve in his place. In other words, he could find a substitute. Some men hired substitutes because their families depended on them. Others did so because they had important jobs. When Grover Cleveland received a message saying he had been drafted, he hired a substitute. He did not want to interrupt his successful career to become a soldier. More importantly, his family still depended on him. His father had died 10 years earlier, and two of his brothers had already volunteered as soldiers in the Union army. Cleveland was left as the main provider to his mother and younger siblings. He paid another man to take his place, which allowed him to continue working as a lawyer.

CHAPTER TWO

LIFE IN POLITICS

In the United States, there are two powerful **political parties:** the **Democrats** and the **Republicans.** All his adult life, Grover Cleveland was a Democrat. But even though he belonged to the Democratic Party and ran for political offices, he believed that government should interfere as little as possible in the lives of the American people. He also thought people should not depend too much on the government for help.

In 1865, Grover Cleveland ran for election for the first time, as district attorney in Erie County. When he did not win, he went to work in a private law office. In 1871, he won his first election, when the people of Erie County chose him as their sheriff. In his new job, he investigated crimes and arrested people who broke the law. He was in charge of the county jail as well. Sheriff Cleveland could be called to a crime scene at any hour of the day or night. From time to time, he faced dangerous criminals.

In 1873, Cleveland's term as sheriff ended. He did not run for office a second time. Instead, he went back to practicing law. Over the years, he became well known to the people of Buffalo. He was known for being honest, firm, kind, and hardworking. He devoted a great deal of time and energy to every job he held.

Cleveland was surprised when Democratic businessmen asked him to run for mayor of Buffalo in 1881. But he agreed to do so and won. Being mayor was a difficult job. Buffalo city officials had not always been honest in the past. Some had cheated the city government out of money. Others had appointed their friends and relatives to city jobs instead of choosing the best people with the most skills. As mayor, Cleveland was a **reformer.** This meant he wanted to clean up the city government. There would be no wrongdoing in the government with Grover Cleveland in charge.

As sheriff, Grover Cleveland hanged two men convicted of violent crimes.

Grover Cleveland practiced law in this office building in Buffalo, New York.

The people of Buffalo described Grover Cleveland as "ugly honest" because he was very blunt. This is a portrait of Cleveland when he was mayor of Buffalo in the early 1880s.

Cleveland's honesty won the respect of other people working for government reform, including officials in the New York State government. Leaders of the state's Democratic Party soon asked Cleveland to run for an even more important office. In 1882, he ran for governor of New York State.

Cleveland won the election and moved to Albany, New York's state capital. As governor, he continued to win praise for his dedication to reform. He fought to stop **corruption** in the state government and in New York City. By nature, Cleveland was **frugal,** meaning he did not like to waste money. He refused to sign into law **bills** that he believed would waste the state's money. Always stubborn, he fought hard for what he thought was right.

While Cleveland was governor, the people of New York learned more about the honest **politician** from Buffalo. They admired Cleveland's accomplishments. So did leaders in the national Democratic Party. In 1884, they asked Cleveland to run for president of the United States. They thought he was an ideal **candidate,** because he was new to politics. Americans seemed to want a reformer in the White House. Democratic leaders hoped Cleveland could win votes not only from Democrats but Republicans as well.

Cleveland won the election for governor without making a single campaign speech. People voted for him because they knew he was an honest man.

As governor of New York, Cleveland made sure that the state government used its money wisely. During this time, Cleveland won such a widespread reputation for honesty, the Democratic Party wanted him to run for president.

As this political cartoon shows, the 1884 presidential campaign was full of "mudslinging"—the candidates ran negative campaigns full of insults and accusations against each other.

The election of 1884 was a very ugly one. The Republican candidate, longtime politician James G. Blaine, had a bad reputation. As a member of Congress, he had been accused of illegal activities. His enemies said he did whatever railroad companies wanted. Some Republicans—a group of reformers who called themselves the Mugwumps—hated Blaine. Democrats called him a continental liar in their campaign slogan.

Terrible things were also said about Grover Cleveland. He was accused of being the father of a young, unmarried woman's child. Cleveland never denied the charges. Many Americans refused to vote for him because of this. But others thought what he did in public office was more important than what he did in his private life.

On Election Day of 1884, Grover Cleveland won by a small number of votes. On March 4, 1885, he was sworn in as president of the United States in Washington, D.C.

Grover Cleveland was not a man of culture. He did not particularly like to listen to music or read novels or poetry. In Buffalo, he often spent the little free time he had in restaurants and saloons or outdoors, hunting and fishing.

THE GREAT NATIONAL FISHING MATCH.

IT'S MINE?

This cartoon shows Grover Cleveland as a fisherman "landing" the presidency, as his opponent (James Blaine) looks on. Cleveland won the election of 1884 and became president the following March.

CORRUPTION IN NEW YORK

In the 1870s and 1880s, there was corruption in the New York State government. Some dishonest officials used their power to earn money for themselves. The situation was especially bad in New York City, where William Marcy Tweed had become the "boss."

Tweed was a member of the city council. He was also the leader of Tammany Hall, an organization that helped immigrants. Tammany Hall found jobs and homes for people who had just arrived in the United States. But it also tried to control New York City's government. Tammany Hall paid voters to use more than one name to cast extra votes in elections. This way, Boss Tweed could make sure the people he supported were elected to office.

Tweed and other government officials also helped their friends find work. If the government had to hire builders, for example, these officials made sure their friends received the jobs. In exchange, the officials demanded a portion of what the government paid the builders for their work. Once Boss Tweed helped a man get a contract to work on a city building. Although it was not a big job, Tweed's friend charged close to two million dollars. Much of that money went into Tweed's own pocket. As governor of New York, Grover Cleveland fought hard to end such corruption. Along the way, he angered some people in the New York government but he won the support of many voters.

CHAPTER THREE

THE FIRST TERM

When he arrived in Washington, D.C., Grover Cleveland immediately set to work. He became one of the hardest-working presidents of all time. Many days he spent more than 12 hours working at his desk. Sometimes he started work at eight o'clock in the morning and did not stop until after eight o'clock at night.

As president, Cleveland continued to work for government reform. One of his major goals was to prevent Congress from favoring special interests—like the railroad companies. He also worked very hard to force Congress to give government jobs only to people who were qualified for them. Under President Chester A. Arthur, Congress had passed the Pendleton Civil Service Act. This law had put in place a "merit system" for government workers. This meant politicians could

When Cleveland became president, few Americans knew who he was. One challenge he faced was earning the respect of Congress.

*When Cleveland arrived in Washington, D.C., for his **inauguration,** it was only his second visit to the capital city. The crowd that gathered for the event was the largest he had ever seen.*

When Cleveland was elected in 1884, he became the first Democrat to win a presidential election since James Buchanan in 1856. Democrats had trouble getting elected because many southerners were Democrats, and for years, people in the North blamed southern Democrats for the Civil War.

no longer hire people simply because they owed them favors; they could not offer jobs to people who had given them money for their election campaigns.

But the Pendleton Civil Service Act had not been enforced. As president, Cleveland went through the lists of employees who worked for the national government. He fired those who had gotten their jobs unfairly. This angered many members of Congress. Some claimed that Cleveland did not have the right to do so. But Cleveland fought back. He pointed out that the U.S. **Constitution** gives the president power to fill government positions.

The American public supported Cleveland. The Senate finally gave in and started to approve the people he chose for government jobs. In 1886, Congress voted to overturn the Tenure of Office Act. This 1867 law had limited the power presidents had to appoint or fire government officials. When it was overturned, it was a victory for Cleveland.

Abraham Lincoln was the 16th president of the United States. William McKinley was the 25th. Grover Cleveland was the only president between those two presidents who did not fight in the Civil War.

President Cleveland (far left) strongly believed that only the most qualified people should be chosen for government jobs. Here he is shown with his cabinet—his group of closest advisors. Every president picks the members of his cabinet.

Cleveland was a decisive president. He vetoed 414 bills in his first term. That was more than double the 204 vetoes cast by all previous presidents combined.

Cleveland had become a powerful president. But as time went on, he was not one to offer his opinion about lawmaking to Congress. He did not suggest ideas for new laws, nor did he discuss bills with members of Congress. If he approved of a bill, he signed it into law. When he did not like a bill, he **vetoed** it. When a president vetoes a bill, he refuses to sign it. This means it does not become a law. Cleveland vetoed hundreds of bills. They would not become law unless two-thirds of Congress voted to **overrule** his veto.

Most often, Cleveland vetoed spending bills. During his presidency, Congress passed hundreds of bills providing **pensions** to Civil War soldiers. Cleveland read every one carefully and then vetoed almost all of them. He knew that many people who applied for these pensions were dishonest. Some had left the army without permission. Others had never even served in the army. Another bill he vetoed would have given money to Western farmers who were being hurt by a drought. A severe lack of rain meant they could not grow any crops. Cleveland believed it was not the job of the national government to provide relief money to people in times like this.

Cleveland looked for other ways to cut government spending. For example, he always paid his own expenses. Earlier presidents had the government pay for things like fancy furnishings for the White House and a sailboat. Cleveland refused to indulge in such luxuries.

In 1886, Cleveland surprised the nation by getting married. He was 49 years old at the time. Before he was married, one of his sisters had acted as first lady.

When he first became president, Cleveland did not have a secretary. He sometimes answered the White House telephone himself.

This political cartoon shows Cleveland shaking hands with an ordinary citizen. Although the president often had difficulty working with Congress, he was popular with the American people.

Before his marriage, Americans knew of Cleveland's friendship with the Folsom family. Many expected Grover Cleveland to marry Frances's mother, Emma, not Frances herself.

Now that role would be filled by his new wife, Frances Folsom. Frances was just 21. She was the daughter of Cleveland's former law partner, who had died 13 years earlier.

Grover Cleveland and Frances Folsom were married in the White House. They invited only a few friends and celebrated in a very quiet manner. In keeping with his frugal nature, Cleveland did not want an expensive wedding. He did make one very romantic gesture, however. He made sure the White House was filled with beautiful flowers.

At age 21, Frances Cleveland was the youngest First Lady in history. She was also one of the most popular. Americans admired her grace and beauty. One member of the White House staff said, "Her very presence threw an air of beauty on the entire surroundings, whatever the occasion or company."

Cleveland liked to hold a public reception at the White House each New Year's Day. After his marriage, these receptions became especially popular. Sometimes 8,000 visitors came. He and Frances tried to shake everyone's hand.

After their marriage, Grover and Frances Cleveland went on a five-day honeymoon to Maryland. Americans were so fascinated by the couple that newspaper reporters followed them. When they returned to Washington, Frances found she had become a celebrity. Nevertheless, the couple tried to lead a quiet

Cleveland was such a hard worker, he took care of business matters even on his wedding day.

life. Cleveland continued to save the government every penny he could. He even discouraged the White House cook from making fancy meals.

Toward the end of his first term, Cleveland asked Congress to lower **tariffs.** President Lincoln had increased these taxes, which were placed on **imports** to help pay for the Civil War. After the war, they protected U.S. companies because they increased

In 1886, France gave the United States a beautiful gift: the Statue of Liberty. President Cleveland dedicated the statue in front of a large, excited crowd that had gathered for the event.

THE DAWES ACT

By the time Cleveland was elected president, Native Americans no longer lived freely wherever they liked on the Western plains. They had lost many battles against the U.S. Army. Most Native Americans were assigned to **reservations**. Life was often difficult on these confined reservations, and Grover Cleveland believed that life would be better for Native Americans if they lived more like most white Americans.

On February 8, 1887, President Cleveland signed the Dawes Act. It was designed to encourage Native Americans to give up their tribal ways, send their children to boarding schools, and own their land as individuals rather than tribes. But the Dawes Act soon proved **devastating** to those it claimed to benefit. Disregarding centuries of tradition, the act transferred land ownership from tribes to individuals. However, if the government decided that these individual landowners were not doing a good enough job farming the land, it took the land away, usually transferring it to white settlers.

Another result of the Dawes Act was that many Native Americans were sent to boarding schools like the one shown below, where they were forbidden to speak in their native tongue or perform tribal rituals. Although Cleveland's intentions were good, the Dawes Act turned out to be a disastrous policy for Native Americans, robbing them of much of their land and culture. Congress **abolished** the act in 1934.

Grover Cleveland did not like the food served at the White House. He wrote the following in a letter: "I must go to dinner, but I wish it was to eat a pickled herring, a Swiss cheese, and a chop at Louis' instead of the French stuff I shall find."

the price of foreign goods. Cleveland thought high tariffs were no longer needed. He pointed out that the government had a great deal of money. He believed that Congress used the extra money to fund unnecessary projects. But Cleveland received little support for his plan. Owners of big businesses complained. So did workers, who believed that tariffs helped keep their wages high because more American goods were sold. As the next election approached, President Cleveland was losing popularity.

This campaign poster for President Grover Cleveland tells of his plan to lower tariffs, which are taxes placed on goods from other countries.

THE PRESIDENTIAL VETO

The U.S. Constitution gives presidents the right to veto any bill passed by Congress. This means that the president can refuse to sign a bill in an attempt to keep it from becoming law. If this happens, the bill is sent back to Congress. Both houses of Congress—the House of Representatives and the Senate—must vote on it again. In order for the bill to become law, two-thirds of the members of Congress must vote in favor of the bill. This is called "overriding" the president's veto. Without enough votes, the bill "dies" and does not become law.

Early presidents like George Washington knew they had the right to veto, but they rarely did so. The presidents' use of the veto increased over time, however. Andrew Jackson used it 12 times. Ulysses S. Grant vetoed more than 90 bills. Grover Cleveland vetoed a total of 584 bills.

CHAPTER FOUR

THE SECOND TERM

In 1888, the Democratic Party asked Grover Cleveland to run for a second term as president, and he agreed. The Republican Party chose Benjamin Harrison as their candidate. He was a hero from the Civil War and the grandson of William Henry Harrison, the nation's ninth president. Benjamin Harrison's campaign favored tariffs. He had the support of workers and American businesses.

When the election took place in November, Grover Cleveland actually won the popular vote. That means more Americans voted for him than for Benjamin Harrison. But Cleveland lost the electoral vote. In the United States, it is the electoral vote—not the popular vote—that determines who wins a presidential election. Each state has a certain number of electoral votes that is determined by its population. The candidate who wins the most popular votes in a state receives all of that state's electoral votes. If the popular election is very close in many states, a candidate can get into office by winning more states even if he or she has won fewer popular votes. That is what happened in the election of 1888.

Grover and Frances Cleveland were shocked and disappointed when Grover did not win this second election. They left Washington right after Benjamin Harrison's inauguration. They moved to New York City. Grover Cleveland went back to work as a lawyer. During that time, the Clevelands had their first child, a little girl named Ruth. They ended up having five children together.

Harrison proved to be a weak president. He did not accomplish much during his term. Democrats realized that they missed Cleveland. In 1892, Cleveland faced Harrison again when the Democrats chose him as their candidate for a third time. At first, it looked as though it would be a close race. But the Republicans had problems. For one thing, the People's Party, a new political party, took votes away from the Republicans. For another thing, toward the end of the campaign, Harrison's wife became very ill. She died just two

Cleveland lost the election of 1888 to Benjamin Harrison. The day of Harrison's inauguration, March 4, 1889, was rainy and cold. Legend has it that Grover Cleveland held an umbrella over Harrison's head as he took the oath of office.

In 1893, during Cleveland's second term as president, the United States experienced the worst depression in its history up to that time. Many Americans became unemployed. This 1893 photograph shows poor people living in shacks in Chicago.

When the Clevelands left the White House in 1889, Mrs. Cleveland asked a servant to take good care of the furniture and decorations. "I want to find everything just as it is now when we come back again," she said. Surprised, the servant asked when she expected to return. "We are coming back just four years from today," she replied.

weeks before election day. By that time, Harrison did not care how the election turned out, and he stopped campaigning. In the end, Cleveland won the election by a large number of votes.

Cleveland's second term was very difficult. Just two months after his inauguration, a **depression** began. For complicated reasons, hundreds of American banks failed, closing their doors. Companies went out of business, too. Workers lost their jobs. Many Americans suddenly became poor. Cleveland tried to help end the depression, but he failed.

During the first year of his second term, Cleveland suffered a personal crisis as well. His doctor told him that he had developed cancer in his mouth. He had a **tumor** that needed to be removed. Cleveland did not want Americans to know he had cancer. He made arrangements to have a surgeon remove the tumor in secret. He sneaked away from the White House to a friend's boat. The surgery was performed there. The operation was a success, and the tumor was removed. But to do so, the surgeon also had to remove a large portion of his upper jaw. Cleveland had it replaced with an artificial rubber jaw, which made it difficult for him to speak. It took months for him to learn to speak clearly again.

Two other very important events took place during Cleveland's second term. Earlier, the Senate had voted to make the islands of Hawaii part of the United States. An agreement had already been written, but Cleveland did not think the United States had a right

Grover Cleveland was a very heavy smoker. He especially enjoyed smoking cigars. This bad habit harmed him. He developed cancer of the mouth.

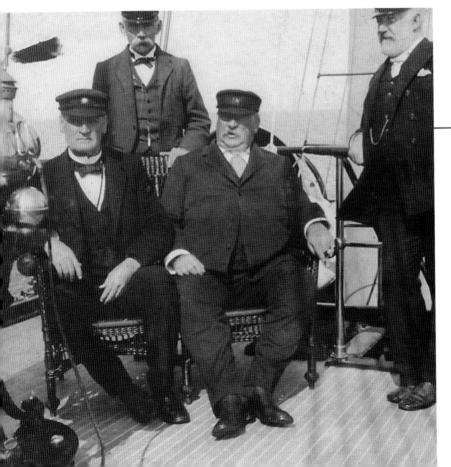

This rare photograph shows President Cleveland on the yacht where his secret jaw surgery was performed in 1893.

President Cleveland's second term was filled with difficult challenges. By the end, he had no interest in seeking another four years in office.

When you play the game of Monopoly®, you may draw a card from the Chance pile that reads "We're off the gold standard, collect $50." Grover Cleveland supported the gold standard, which meant that the federal government could issue only as much paper money as it had in gold in the Treasury. The United States was on the gold standard until 1933.

to take over Hawaii. He refused to sign the agreement. Because of Cleveland, Hawaii would not become a U.S. **territory** until 1900. It finally became the 50th state in 1959.

In 1894, Cleveland used his presidential power yet again. He sent soldiers to end the Pullman **strike** in Chicago. Workers were demanding better treatment from the Pullman Car Company, which made railroad cars. Cleveland's decision to end the strike made him unpopular with American workers. They felt he had sided with rich business owners. In congressional elections held in November of 1894, Republicans won many seats in the Senate and the House. After that, Cleveland no longer had the tremendous power he once enjoyed.

Americans lost faith in Cleveland as his second term wore on. In 1896, the Democratic Party chose a man named William Jennings Bryan to run for president instead of Grover Cleveland. Cleveland was relieved to be leaving the presidency with all its responsibilities. He retired to Princeton, New Jersey in 1897.

Toward the end of his presidency, Grover Cleveland became so unpopular, he ordered that the White House gates be locked. This was to keep out angry Americans.

After Cleveland's presidency, he and his family moved to Princeton, New Jersey. Shown in this photograph (from left to right) are Esther, Francis, Mrs. Frances Cleveland, Marion, Richard, and Grover Cleveland. The family's first child, Ruth, had died of a serious illness.

Grover Cleveland remained active in his later years. Here he is shown (at right) fishing with friends in 1904.

Because Cleveland insisted that doctors treat his cancer in secret, Americans did not learn of it until 1917—nine years after his death.

Even in retirement, Cleveland remained in the public eye. He wrote books and articles and made speeches. He did a great deal of work for Princeton University, raising funds and speaking to students. But, after years of nonstop work, he also let himself take time off to relax. He spent time with Frances and their children. He also enjoyed two of his favorite pastimes, fishing and hunting.

In his late sixties, Cleveland began to have health problems and slowed down. His illnesses became more and more serious. He finally died at his home on June 24, 1908, at the age of 71. The nation mourned his death. Today many Americans consider Cleveland to have been a fine president, and he is admired for his honesty, dedication, and hard work.

THE PULLMAN STRIKE

George Pullman was a rich businessman who owned the
Pullman Car Company, located near Chicago. It made railroad
cars to carry passengers. Train travel became very popular
after the transcontinental railroad was finished in 1869.
Pullman sleeping cars were fancy and comfortable. They
included seats that turned into beds. Additional beds pulled
down from the ceiling. Other features of Pullman cars included
beautiful wood panels, huge mirrors, and thick, soft carpets.

The Pullman Car Company employed many workers. Mr.
Pullman built a town just for them. This was what was known
as a company town. Mr. Pullman provided workers with schools,
parks, a store, and a library—but he also set many rules. Many
workers became dissatisfied living there. They became especially
angry after Mr. Pullman cut their
wages but did not lower their rent.

Thousands of his workers joined
the American Railway Union and went
on strike. Unions are groups of workers
who band together to demand better
wages or improved working conditions.
Soon, about 120,000 workers were
on strike. Although the strike remained
peaceful, it stopped nearly all rail traffic.

Finally, the U.S. government
ordered the union to make its members
go back to work. When the union
refused, President Cleveland sent
thousands of soldiers to take care of the problem. When the
troops arrived, union members rioted. As the violence grew
serious, soldiers attacked the workers. In the end, 13 people
died and more than 50 were wounded. The union gave in and
called off the strike. Workers were forced to return to work.

Although the soldiers ended the strike, it caused
serious problems in the workforce. The decision to send
troops angered many working Americans. They believed
that the U.S. government and wealthy business owners
were working together to enslave poor Americans.

1830	1840	1850	1860	1870

1837
Grover Cleveland is born on March 18 in Caldwell, New Jersey.

1843
Cleveland starts school at age six.

1853
Cleveland drops out of school at age 16 to help support his family after his father dies.

1855
Cleveland settles in Buffalo, New York. He works on his uncle's farm and then in a lawyer's office as a clerk.

1859
Cleveland passes the bar exam and becomes a lawyer.

1861
The Civil War begins. Two of Grover Cleveland's brothers enlist as volunteers in the Union army.

1863
Grover Cleveland becomes an assistant district attorney for Erie County, New York. He is drafted into the Union army but hires a substitute to fight in his place.

1865
Grover Cleveland loses his first election when he runs for the office of district attorney.

1871
Grover Cleveland is elected sheriff of Erie County.

1873
Cleveland's term as sheriff ends. He goes back to work as an attorney in a law office.

1881
Cleveland is elected mayor of Buffalo, New York.

1882
After only one year as mayor of Buffalo, Cleveland is elected governor of New York.

1883
Cleveland begins his duties as governor of New York.

1884
Cleveland is elected president of the United States.

1885
In March, Cleveland is inaugurated president and begins his duties. During his first year in office, he fights with Congress over who should fill government positions.

1886
Congress admits that Cleveland has the right to make appointments to political office and overturns the Tenure of Office Act. This represents an important victory for Cleveland. Cleveland marries Frances Folsom in the White House on June 2.

1887
Cleveland becomes involved in a fight with Congress over high tariffs. He wants them reduced, but business leaders and workers do not.

1888
Cleveland runs for reelection. He is shocked when he loses. His stand on tariffs is the major cause for the loss.

1889
Benjamin Harrison is sworn in as the new president. Grover and Frances Cleveland move to New York City. He returns to work as an attorney.

1892
Cleveland runs for president a third time. He beats his opponent, Benjamin Harrison, who had defeated him four years earlier.

1893
Cleveland begins his second term as president. A depression begins. Many businesses close, and people lose their jobs. Although the government wants to make Hawaii a U.S. territory, Cleveland refuses to agree. Cleveland is diagnosed with cancer of the mouth, and a tumor is removed in secret.

1894
Cleveland exerts his presidential power and sends American troops to end the Pullman strike. This makes him unpopular with the public. In the fall election, Republicans are elected to many seats in Congress, replacing Democrats. Cleveland loses much of his power after the elections.

1896
Cleveland is not chosen to run for a third term as president. William McKinley is elected the 25th president.

1897
After McKinley is inaugurated, Cleveland retires to private life.

1908
After more than 10 years in retirement, Grover Cleveland dies at home on June 24 at the age of 71.

GLOSSARY

abolished (uh-BOHL-isht) If something is abolished, it has been stopped or ended. Congress eventually abolished the Dawes Act.

appointed (uh-POYN-ted) When people are appointed, they are asked by an important official to fill a position. Cleveland was appointed assistant district attorney of Erie County.

bills (BILZ) Bills are ideas for new laws that are presented to a group of lawmakers. Cleveland refused to sign bills that he felt were a waste of the government's money.

campaign (kam-PAYN) A campaign is the process of running for an election, including activities such as giving speeches or attending rallies. Cleveland won the election of 1884 after a tough campaign.

candidate (KAN-dih-det) A candidate is a person running in an election. Members of the Democratic Party thought Cleveland would make an excellent presidential candidate in 1884.

consecutive (kuhn-SEK-yuh-tiv) Consecutive means following one after the other. Grover Cleveland's presidential terms were not consecutive—he served one term, then Benjamin Harrison served a term, and then Cleveland served a second term.

constitution (kon-stih-TOO-shun) A constitution is the set of basic principles that govern a state, country, or society. The U.S. Constitution gives the president the power to fill government positions.

corruption (kuh-RUP-shun) Corruption is dishonesty. Cleveland fought corruption in the government.

Democrats (DEM-uh-kratz) Democrats are members of the Democratic political party, one of the two major political parties in the United States. Cleveland belonged to the Democratic Party.

depression (deh-PRESH-un) A depression is a period of time in which there is little business activity, and many people are out of work. A depression began shortly after Cleveland entered office in 1893.

devastating (DEV-uh-stayt-ing) Actions that destroy something or someone are devastating. The Dawes Act was devastating to Native Americans.

frugal (FROO-guhl) Frugal means using money or other resources sparingly. Grover Cleveland was frugal.

immigrant (IM-ih-grent) An immigrant is a person who moves to a new country. Tammany Hall was a New York organization that helped immigrants to find work.

imports (IM-portz) Imports are goods brought from one country to another. Cleveland felt that higher taxes on imports were not needed.

inauguration (ih-nawg-yuh-RAY-shun) An inauguration is the ceremony that takes place when a new president begins a term. Cleveland's first inauguration took place March 4, 1885.

overrule (oh-ver-ROOL) If Congress votes to overrule, it does not accept a president's veto. For a bill to become law, two-thirds of both houses of Congress must vote to overrule the veto.

pensions (PEN-shunz) Pensions are regular payments made to someone who is retired. The government paid pensions to soldiers who fought in the Civil War.

political parties (puh-LIT-ih-kul PAR-teez) Political parties are groups of people who share similar ideas about how to run a government. The Democratic Party is one of the two most powerful political parties in the United States.

politician (pawl-ih-TISH-un) A politician is a person who holds an office in government. Cleveland was a politician.

politics (PAWL-ih-tiks) Politics refers to the actions and practices of the government. Cleveland became interested in politics when he moved to Buffalo, New York.

reformer (ree-FORM-uhr) A reformer is a person who makes changes in the way government is run. Cleveland was considered a reformer.

Republicans (ree-PUB-lih-kinz) Republicans belong to the Republican Party, one of the two major U.S. political parties. When Cleveland ran for president, he ran against Republican candidates.

reputation (rep-yoo-TAY-shun) A reputation is one's worth or character, as judged by other people. Cleveland had a reputation for being a good lawyer.

reservations (rez-uhr-VAY-shuns) Reservations are land that the U.S. government has set aside for Native Americans to live on. Many Native Americans were moved to reservations in the late 1800s.

strike (STRYK) A strike is when workers quit working hoping to force an employer to meet a demand. Workers at the Pullman Car Company went on strike to ask for better wages.

tariffs (TAYR-ifs) Tariffs are taxes on goods that are imported from other countries. Cleveland wanted to lower tariffs.

territory (TAYR-uh-tor-ee) A territory is a land or region, especially land that belongs to a government. Cleveland did not want Hawaii to become a U.S. territory.

tumor (TOO-mur) A tumor is an abnormal growth of cells or tissue in the body. Cleveland had a tumor in his mouth.

Union (YOON-yen) The Union is another name for the United States of America. During the Civil War, the North was called the Union. A Union can also be a group of workers who have banded together to demand better wages or improved working conditions.

vetoed (VEE-tohd) If a president rejected a bill that has been passed by Congress, he or she vetoed it. Cleveland vetoed hundreds of bills.

THE UNITED STATES GOVERNMENT

The United States government is divided into three equal branches: the executive, the legislative, and the judicial. This division helps prevent abuses of power because each branch has to answer to the other two. No one branch can become too powerful.

EXECUTIVE BRANCH

President
Vice President
Departments

The job of the executive branch is to enforce the laws. It is headed by the president, who serves as the spokesperson for the United States around the world. The president signs bills into law and appoints important officials such as federal judges. He or she is also the commander in chief of the U.S. military. The president is assisted by the vice president, who takes over if the president dies or cannot carry out the duties of the office.

The executive branch also includes various departments, each focused on a specific topic. They include the Defense Department, the Justice Department, and the Agriculture Department. The department heads, along with other officials such as the vice president, serve as the president's closest advisers, called the cabinet.

LEGISLATIVE BRANCH

Congress
Senate and
House of Representatives

The job of the legislative branch is to make the laws. It consists of Congress, which is divided into two parts: the Senate and the House of Representatives. The Senate has 100 members, and the House of Representatives has 435 members. Each state has two senators. The number of representatives a state has varies depending on the state's population.

Besides making laws, Congress also passes budgets and enacts taxes. In addition, it is responsible for declaring war, maintaining the military, and regulating trade with other countries.

JUDICIAL BRANCH

Supreme Court
Courts of Appeals
District Courts

The job of the judicial branch is to interpret the laws. It consists of the nation's federal courts. Trials are held in district courts. During trials, judges must decide what laws mean and how they apply. Courts of appeals review the decisions made in district courts.

The nation's highest court is the Supreme Court. If someone disagrees with a court of appeals ruling, he or she can ask the Supreme Court to review it. The Supreme Court may refuse. The Supreme Court makes sure that decisions and laws do not violate the Constitution.

CHOOSING
THE PRESIDENT

It may seem odd, but American voters don't elect the president directly. Instead, the president is chosen using what is called the Electoral College.

Each state gets as many votes in the Electoral College as its combined total of senators and representatives in Congress. For example, Iowa has two senators and five representatives, so it gets seven electoral votes. Although the District of Columbia does not have any voting members in Congress, it gets three electoral votes. Usually, the candidate who wins the most votes in any given state receives all of that state's electoral votes.

To become president, a candidate must get more than half of the Electoral College votes. There are a total of 538 votes in the Electoral College, so a candidate needs 270 votes to win. If nobody receives 270 Electoral College votes, the House of Representatives chooses the president.

With the Electoral College system, the person who receives the most votes nationwide does not always receive the most electoral votes. This happened most recently in 2000, when Al Gore received half a million more national votes than George W. Bush. Bush became president because he had more Electoral College votes.

THE WHITE HOUSE

The White House is the official home of the president of the United States. It is located at 1600 Pennsylvania Avenue NW in Washington, D.C. In 1792, a contest was held to select the architect who would design the president's home. James Hoban won. Construction took eight years.

The first president, George Washington, never lived in the White House. The second president, John Adams, moved into the house in 1800, though the inside was not yet complete. During the War of 1812, British soldiers burned down much of the White House. It was rebuilt several years later.

The White House was changed through the years. Porches were added, and President Theodore Roosevelt added the West Wing. President William Taft changed the shape of the presidential office, making it into the famous Oval Office. While Harry Truman was president, the old house was discovered to be structurally weak. All the walls were reinforced with steel, and the rooms were rebuilt.

Today, the White House has 132 rooms (including 35 bathrooms), 28 fireplaces, and 3 elevators. It takes 570 gallons of paint to cover the outside of the six-story building. The White House provides the president with many ways to relax. It includes a putting green, a jogging track, a swimming pool, a tennis court, and beautifully landscaped gardens. The White House also has a movie theater, a billiard room, and a one-lane bowling alley.

PRESIDENTIAL PERKS

The job of president of the United States is challenging. It is probably one of the most stressful jobs in the world. Because of this, presidents are paid well, though not nearly as well as the leaders of large corporations. In 2007, the president earned $400,000 a year. Presidents also receive extra benefits that make the demanding job a little more appealing.

★ **Camp David:** In the 1940s, President Franklin D. Roosevelt chose this heavily wooded spot in the mountains of Maryland to be the presidential retreat, where presidents can relax. Even though it is a retreat, world business is conducted there. Most famously, President Jimmy Carter met with Middle Eastern leaders at Camp David in 1978. The result was a peace agreement between Israel and Egypt.

★ *Air Force One:* The president flies on a jet called *Air Force One*. It is a Boeing 747-200B that has been modified to meet the president's needs.

Air Force One is the size of a large home. It is equipped with a dining room, sleeping quarters, a conference room, and office space. It also has two kitchens that can provide food for up to 50 people.

★ **The Secret Service:** While not the most glamorous of the president's perks, the Secret Service is one of the most important. The Secret Service is a group of highly trained agents who protect the president and the president's family.

★ **The Presidential State Car:** The presidential limousine is a stretch Cadillac DTS.

It has been armored to protect the president in case of attack. Inside the plush car are a foldaway desk, an entertainment center, and a communications console.

★ **The Food:** The White House has five chefs who will make any food the president wants. The White House also has an extensive wine collection.

★ **Retirement:** A former president receives a pension, or retirement pay, of just under $180,000 a year. Former presidents also receive Secret Service protection for the rest of their lives.

FACTS

QUALIFICATIONS

To run for president, a candidate must

* be at least 35 years old
* be a citizen who was born in the United States
* have lived in the United States for 14 years

TERM OF OFFICE

A president's term of office is four years.
No president can stay in office for more than two terms.

ELECTION DATE

The presidential election takes place every four years on the first Tuesday of November.

INAUGURATION DATE

Presidents are inaugurated on January 20.

OATH OF OFFICE

I do solemnly swear I will faithfully execute the office of the President of the United States and will to the best of my ability preserve, protect, and defend the Constitution of the United States.

WRITE A LETTER TO THE PRESIDENT

One of the best things about being a U.S. citizen is that Americans get to participate in their government. They can speak out if they feel government leaders aren't doing their jobs. They can also praise leaders who are going the extra mile. Do you have something you'd like the president to do? Should the president worry more about the environment and encourage people to recycle? Should the government spend more money on our schools? You can write a letter to the president to say how you feel!

1600 Pennsylvania Avenue
Washington, D.C. 20500
You can even send an e-mail to: president@whitehouse.gov

BOOKS

Cleveland, Grover. *Good Citizenship.* Bedford, MA: Applewood Books, 1996.

Hakim, Joy. *Age of Extremes.* New York: Oxford University Press, 2003.

Hakim, Joy. *Reconstructing America.* New York: Oxford University Press, 2003.

Markel, Rita J. *Grover Cleveland.* Minneapolis: Twenty-First Century Books, 2007.

Ochester, Betsy. *Grover Cleveland: America's 22nd and 24th President.* New York: Children's Press, 2004.

Tecco, Betsy Dru. *How to Draw the Life and Times of Grover Cleveland.* New York: PowerKids Press, 2006.

Williams, Jean Kinney. *Grover Cleveland.* Minneapolis: Compass Point Books, 2003.

VIDEOS

The American President. DVD, VHS (Alexandria, VA: PBS Home Video, 2000).

The History Channel Presents The Presidents. DVD (New York: A&E Home Video, 2005).

National Geographic's Inside the White House. DVD (Washington, D.C.: National Geographic Video, 2003).

INTERNET SITES

Visit our Web page for lots of links about Grover Cleveland and other U.S. presidents:

http://www.childsworld.com/links

Note to Parents, Teachers, and Librarians: We routinely verify our Web links to make sure they are safe, active sites—so encourage your readers to check them out!

INDEX